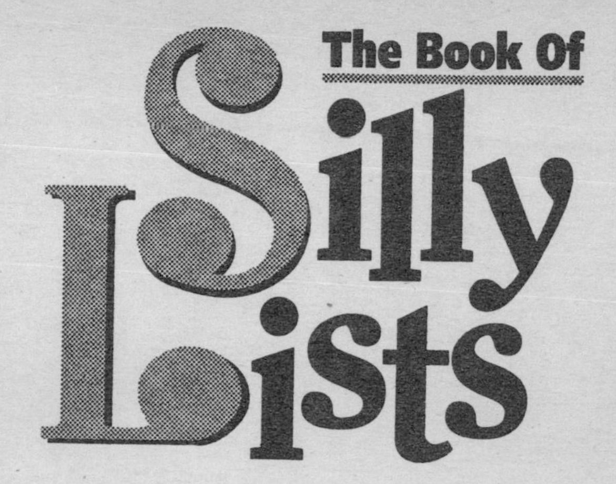

By Patrick M. Reynolds

Watermill Press

Library of Congress Cataloging-in-Publication Data

Reynolds, Patrick M.
The book of silly lists / written by Patrick M. Reynolds.
p. cm.
Summary: A compilation of lists of such things as plants that eat animals, youngest presidents, animals with pockets, and common last names.
ISBN 0-89375-354-8 (pbk.)
1. Wit and humor, Juvenile. [1. Curiosities and wonders.]
I. Title.
PN6163.R46 1993
031.02—dc20 92-38660

Illustrated by Patrick M. Reynolds and Aija Janums
Cover illustration by Rod Gonzalez

Printed in the United States of America.
10 9 8 7 6 5 4 3 2 1

4 Plants that eat animals*

Venus's-flytrap
Butterwort
Sundew
Pitcher plant

*Mostly insects

21 Unusual U.S. place names

Accident, Maryland

Antlers, Oklahoma

Bat Cave, North Carolina

Bigfoot, Texas

Burnt Corn, Alabama

Cement, Oklahoma

Crooks, South Dakota

Decoy, Kentucky

Embarrass, Minnesota
(and one in Wisconsin)

Fishtail, Montana

Frostproof, Florida

Good Luck, Maryland

Goodnight, Texas

Gross, Nebraska

Igloo, South Dakota
Money, Mississippi
Pie Town, New Mexico
Tincup, Colorado
Truth or Consequences, New Mexico
Uncertain, Texas

SANTA CLAUS, INDIANA
(and one in Georgia)

4 Items of clothing named after places

Clothing:	Named after:
Argyle socks	Argyll, a county in Scotland
Ascot	a village in England
Bikini	an island in the Pacific Ocean
Tuxedo	a village in New York

5 Tricky tongue twisters

1. Peter Piper picked a peck of pickled peppers.

2. She sells seashells by the seashore.

3. Rubber baby buggy bumpers.

4. How much wood would a woodchuck chuck, if a woodchuck could chuck wood?

5. The sixth sick sheik's sixth sheep's sick.

25 Original names of famous people

Famous person:	Original name:
Robbie Benson	*Robert Segal*
Morgan Brittany	*Suzanne Cupito*
Nicholas Cage	*Nicholas Coppola*
Cher	*Cherilyn Sarkisian*
David Copperfield	*David Kotkin*
Tom Cruise	*Thomas Mopother*
Rodney Dangerfield	*Jacob Cohen*
Sheena Easton	*Sheena Shirley Orr*
Morgan Fairchild	*Patsy McClenny*
Crystal Gayle	*Brenda Gayle Webb*
Barbara Hershey	*Barbara Herzstine*
Elton John	*Reginald Dwight*

Famous person:	**Original name:**
Don Johnson	*Donald Wayne*
Michael Keaton	*Michael Douglas*
Michael Landon	*Eugene Orowitz*
Bruce Lee	*Lee Yuen Kam*
Madonna	*Madonna Louise Ciccone*
Prince	*Prince Rogers Nelson*
Joan Rivers	*Joan Sandra Molinsky*
Susan Sarandon	*Susan Tomaling*
Jane Seymour	*Joyce Frankenberg*
Sting	*Gordon Sumner*
Tina Turner	*Annie Mae Bullock*
Gene Wilder	*Jerome Silberman*
Stevie Wonder	*Stevland Morris*

6 Unusual phobias, or fears

Name of phobia:	**Fear of:**
Clinophobia	Going to bed
Gephydrophobia	Crossing a bridge
Musophobia	Mice
Pogonophobia	Beards
Scholionophobia	School

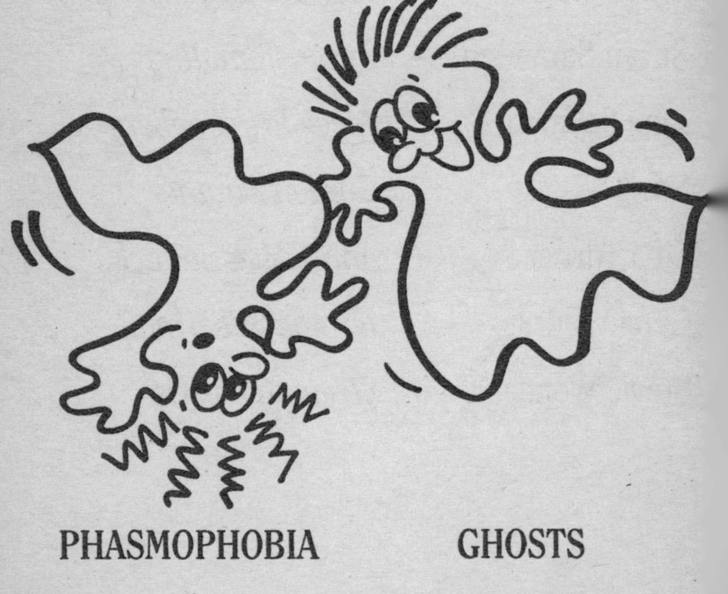

Branch Avenue Bridge
To Be Fixed Before Fall
— *Providence (Rhode Island) Evening Bulletin*

Tuna Biting Off Washington Coast
— *Seattle (Washington) Post-Intelligencer*

Fish & Game To Hold Annual Elections
— *Berkshire Courier, Great Barrington, Massachusetts*

10 Towns with unusual "body" names

Bone, Idaho

Chin, Alberta

Ear Falls, Ontario

Elbow, Saskatchewan

Eye, England

Eyebrow, Saskatchewan

Finger, Tennessee

Footville, Ohio (and one in Wisconsin)

Nose, Japan

Tongue, Scotland

10 Towns with unusual animal names

Alligator, Mississippi

Beagle, Kansas

Bee, Nebraska

Blackbird, Delaware

Canary, Oregon

Dinosaur, Colorado

Moose, Wyoming

Penguin, Tasmania

Porcupine, South Dakota (and one in Ontario)

Trout, Louisiana (and one in West Virginia)

8 Mammals that live in the ocean

Dolphin

Porpoise

Whale

Seal

Sea lion

Walrus

Manatee

Dugong

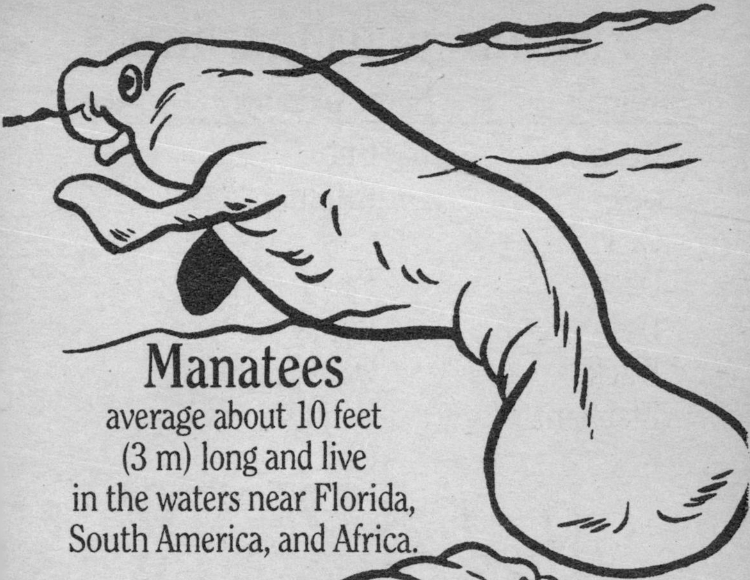

Manatees

average about 10 feet
(3 m) long and live
in the waters near Florida,
South America, and Africa.

Dugongs

have a different tail than
manatees and live in the
Indian Ocean and
as far south as Australia.

22 Names of baby animals

Animal:	Name of baby:
Bear	Cub
Cat	Kitten
Cow	Calf
Deer	Fawn
Dog	Puppy
Duck	Duckling
Elephant	Calf
Fox	Cub

Animal:	Name of baby:
Goat	Kid
Goose	Gosling
Horse	Colt
Kangaroo	Joey
Lion	Cub
Moose	Calf
Oyster	Spat
Seal	Pup
Sheep	Lamb
Swan	Cygnet
Tiger	Cub
Turkey	Poult
Whale	Calf
Wolf	Pup

9 Little creatures of folklore and fairy tales

Brownies

Elves

Genies

Gnomes

Goblins

Gremlins

Leprechauns

Pixies

Trolls

6 U.S. presidents named James

The most common first name among U.S. presidents is James.

James Madison

James Monroe

James K. Polk

James Buchanan

James Garfield

James Earl (Jimmy) Carter

10 Knock-knock jokes

Knock-knock.
Who's there?
Ivana.
Ivana who?
Ivana go home!

Knock-knock.
Who's there?
Anita.
Anita who?
Anita drink of water.

Knock-knock.
Who's there?
Police.
Police who?
Police open the door. I'm tired of knocking.

Knock-knock.
Who's there?
Leif.
Leif who?
Leif me alone.

Knock-knock.
Who's there?
Cows go.
Cows go who?
Cows go moo, not who.

Knock, knock.
Who's there?
Orange.
Orange who?
Orange you glad to see me?

Knock, knock.
Who's there?
Turnip.
Turnip who?
Turnip the radio —
I can't hear it.

Knock-knock.
Who's there?
Little old lady.
Little old lady who?
I didn't know you
could yodel.

Knock-knock.
Who's there?
Eileen.
Eileen who?
Eileen on your
doorbell, but it
doesn't ring.

Ring, ring.
Who's there?
Hurd.
Hurd who?
Hurd my hand,
can't knock.

10 Animals with pockets

Bandicoot

Cuscus

Echidna

Kangaroo

Koala

Opossum

Sea horse

Tasmanian devil

Wallaroo

Wombat

5 of the most common apples

There are thousands of kinds of apples, but here are 5 of the most commonly grown ones:

Delicious

Golden Delicious

McIntosh

Rome Beauty

Jonathan

2 Mammals that lay eggs

Echidna or spiny anteater

Duck-billed platypus

15 Unusual Canadian place names

Cereal, Alberta

Five Fingers, New Brunswick

Furry Creek, British Columbia

Ha! Ha! (lake), Quebec

Hairy Hill, Alberta

Happy Adventure, Newfoundland

Heart's Content, Newfoundland

Mistake Creek, Northwest Territories

Moonbeam, Ontario

Moose Factory, Ontario

Onion Lake, Saskatchewan

Pickle Lake, Ontario

Tiny, Saskatchewan

Wrong (lake), Manitoba

DOG POUND, ALBERTA

4 Famous "sea serpents" some people claim to have seen

Creature:	Home:
The Loch Ness Monster ("Nessie")	Loch Ness, Scotland
Champ	Lake Champlain, USA
Chessie	Chesapeake Bay, USA
Ogopogo	Okanagan Lake, British Columbia, Canada

NESSIE

14 Mountains named Blue

"Purple mountain majesties" is a famous phrase in the song "America the Beautiful." Actually, there are no mountains anywhere in the world named Purple, but there are fourteen mountains named Blue! You can climb them in:

Arkansas
Colorado
Jamaica
Maine
Montana
New Brunswick, Canada
Newfoundland, Canada
New Hampshire
New Mexico
New South Wales, Australia
New York
Oregon
Pennsylvania
Washington

9 Land animals that weigh over 500 pounds (225 kilograms)

Elephant
Giraffe
Kodiak bear
Moose
Polar bear
Rhinoceros
Southern elephant seal
Walrus

HIPPOPOTAMUS

19 Animals with horns or antlers

Antelope

Argali

Bighorn sheep

Bison

Buffalo

Chamois

Eland

Elk

Gazelle

Giraffe

Gnu

Impala

Moose

Musk ox

Oryx

Reindeer

Rocky Mountain goat

Waterbuck

YAK

5 Animals people ride

Camel

Donkey

Elephant

Horse

Mule

A Dromedary is a one-humped camel; a Bactrian is a two-humped camel.

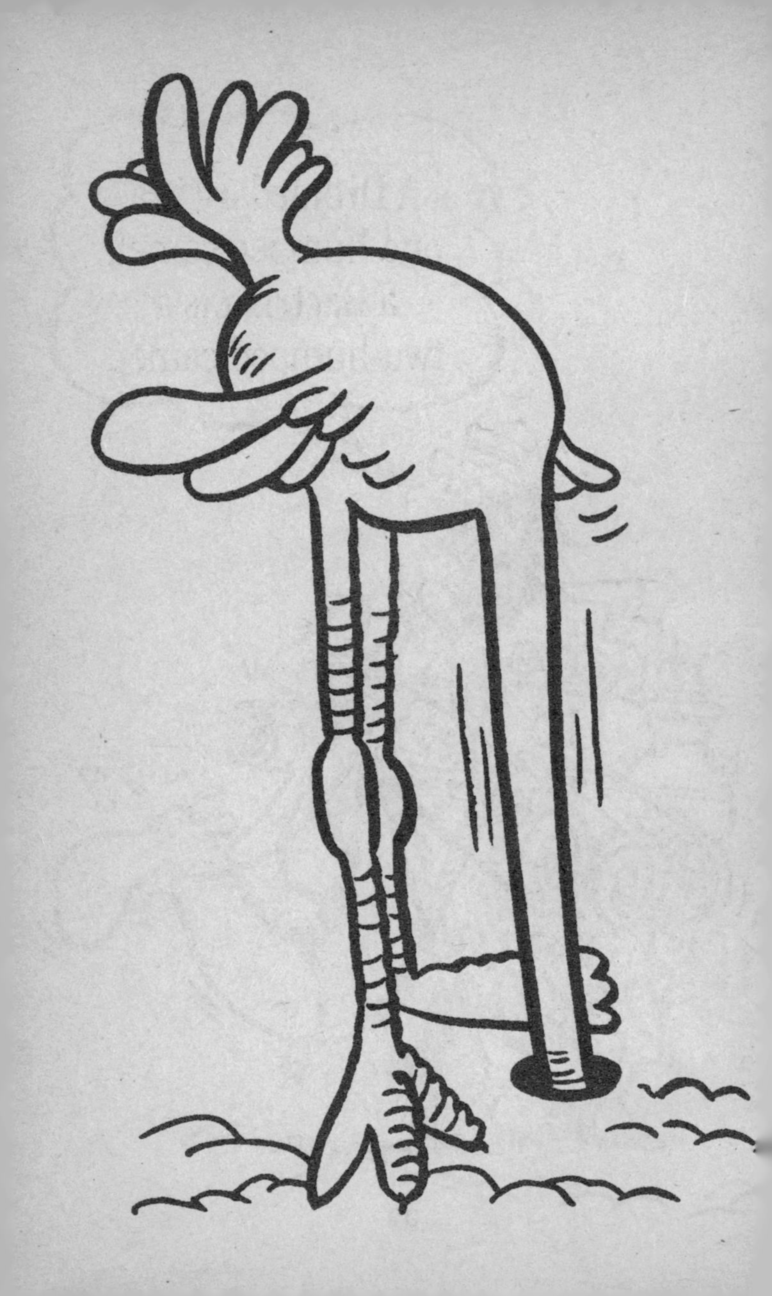

7 Birds that can't fly

Emu

Cassowary

Galapagos cormorant

Penguin

Rhea

18 Words that are spelled the same way both backward and forward

deed
did
eve
ewe
eye
level
madam
mum
noon
nun
peep
pop
pup
radar
rotor
solos
toot
tot

10 Most common U.S. last names

1. Smith
2. Johnson
3. Williams
4. Brown
5. Jones
6. Miller
7. Davis
8. Martin
9. Anderson
10. Wilson

5 Breeds of dogs that bite the least

Golden retriever

Labrador retriever

Shetland sheepdog

Old English sheepdog

Welsh terrier

5 Breeds of dogs that bite the most

German shepherd

Chow

Poodle

Italian bulldog

Fox terrier

OLD ENGLISH SHEEPDOG

6 Tiny places to live

Vatican City State
(only 0.17 square mile/.44 km)

Monaco
(only 0.7 square mile/1.82 square km)

Nauru
(only 8 square miles/20.8 square km)

Tuvalu
(only 10 square miles/26 square km)

San Marino
(only 23.5 square miles/61 square km)

Liechtenstein
(only 61 square miles/158.6 square km)

4 U.S. states whose name and capital begin with the same letter

State:	Capital:
Delaware	Dover
Hawaii	Honolulu
Indiana	Indianapolis
Oklahoma	Oklahoma City

2 Youngest U.S. presidents

Teddy Roosevelt

42 years, 322 days old when he assumed office.

John F. Kennedy

43 years, 236 days old when inaugurated.

3 Heaviest U.S. presidents

William Howard Taft
354 pounds (159 kg);
6 feet (183 cm) tall.

Grover Cleveland
260 pounds (117 kg);
5 feet, 10 inches (178 cm) tall.

Lyndon Baines Johnson
200 pounds (90 kg);
6 feet, 3 inches (191 cm) tall.

TAFT

6 Oldest U.S. presidents

Ronald Reagan
77 years, 348 days old
when he left office.

Dwight D. Eisenhower
70 years, 98 days old
when he left office.

Andrew Jackson
69 years, 354 days old
when he left office.

James Buchanan
69 years, 315 days old
when he left office.

George Bush
68 years, 222 days old
when he left office.

William Henry Harrison

68 years, 54 days old when he died in office after serving only 32 days.

3 Shortest U.S. presidents

James Madison
5 feet, 4 inches
(163 cm)

Martin Van Buren
and
Benjamin Harrison
were both 5 feet, 6 inches
(168 cm)

JAMES MADISON

3 Tallest U.S. presidents

Abraham Lincoln
6 feet, 4 inches
(193 cm)

Lyndon Baines Johnson
6 feet, 3 inches
(191 cm)

Thomas Jefferson
6 feet, $2\frac{1}{2}$ inches
(189 cm)

ABRAHAM LINCOLN

9 Former occupations of U.S. presidents

President:	Former occupation:
George Washington	Surveyor, planter
Andrew Johnson	Tailor
Woodrow Wilson	Teacher
Theodore Roosevelt	Rancher
Warren G. Harding	Newspaper editor
Herbert Hoover	Engineer
Jimmy Carter	Peanut farmer
Ronald Reagan	Actor
George Bush	Oilman

14 Presidential nicknames:

Nickname:	President:
"Father of His Country"	George Washington
"Man of the People"	Thomas Jefferson
"The Little Magician"	Martin Van Buren
"Accidental President"	John Tyler
"The Dark Horse"	James K. Polk
"His Accidency"	Millard Fillmore
"Handsome Frank"	Franklin Pierce
"Honest Abe"	Abraham Lincoln
"United States"	Ulysses S. Grant
"Fraud President"	Rutherford B. Hayes
"Uncle Jumbo"	Grover Cleveland
"Big Bill"	William Howard Taft
"The Professor"	Woodrow Wilson
"The Great Communicator"	Ronald Reagan

5 Nice superstitions

If the bottom of your foot itches,
you will be taking a trip.

If you have a lot of hair on your arms,
you will be rich.

If a cricket comes and stays in your house,
you will have good luck and a happy home.

If you find a four-leaf clover,
you will have good luck.
For even better luck, wear it in your shoe.

If you get an itch on your upper lip,
you will be kissed by someone tall.

11 Places in the world named Warsaw

Many people know that Warsaw is the capital of Poland. But did you know there are at least 11 other cities or towns in the world also named Warsaw? You can visit them in:

Illinois

Indiana

Kentucky

Minnesota

Missouri

New York

North Carolina

North Dakota

Ohio

Ontario, Canada

Virginia

4 Seas named after a color

Black Sea

Red Sea

White Sea

Yellow Sea

4 Unusual lake names

Lake Cadibarrawirracanna, South Australia

Lake Disappointment, Australia
(and one in Newfoundland, Canada)

Mooselookmeguntic Lake, Maine

POSSUM KINGDOM LAKE, TEXAS

10 Fancy names for collectors

Fancy name:	Collects:
archtophilist	teddy bears
bibliophilist	books
copoclephilist	key rings
deltiologist	postcards
philographist	autographs
phonophile	phonograph records
plangonologist	dolls
receptarist	recipes
vecturist	subway tokens
vexillologist	flags

7 Speedy animals

Black mamba snake
(can slither 20 mph/32 kph)

Dragonfly
(can fly 36 mph/58 kph)

Greyhound
(can run 39 mph/62 kph)

Quarter horse
(can run 47.5 mph/76 kph)

Sailfish
(can swim 68 mph/109 kph)

Cheetah
(can run 70 mph/112 kph)

Peregrine falcon
(can swoop 217 mph/347 kph)